HISTORY IN DEPTH

HENRY VIII AND THE DISSOLUTION OF THE MONASTERIES

S.M. Harrison

Head of Humanities, Knutsford County High School, Cheshire

M
MACMILLAN
EDUCATION

To Katy

First published 1985
Reprinted 1985, 1988

Published by
MACMILLAN EDUCATION LTD
Houndmills, Basingstoke, Hampshire RG21 2XS
and London
Companies and representatives
throughout the world

Printed in Hong Kong

British Library Cataloguing in Publication Data
Harrison, Scott
Henry VIII and the dissolution of the
monasteries.—(History in depth)
1. Monasticism and religious orders—England
—History 2. Reformation—England
I. Title II. Series
271′.00942   BX2592
ISBN 0-333-36540-2

Cover illustration courtesy of Aerofilms

CONTENTS

Acknowledgements

The author and publishers wish to acknowledge the
following photograph sources:

Reproduced with kind permission of Her Majesty the
Queen pp 12, 13 top. BBC Hulton Picture Library pp 38,
44; British Library p 13 bottom; British Museum p 51;
by kind permission of Baroness Herries p 39; City of
Bristol Museum & Art Gallery p 46; Crown Copyright –
reproduced with permission of the Controller of H.M.S.O.
pp 11, 14, 25, 28, 32, 41, 48, 50; A.F. Kersting pp 6, 7 right,
52, 53; Magdalene College, Cambridge p 15; Mansell
Collection p 22; National Portrait Gallery, London pp 9,
17, 18, 19, 21, 55; Pitkin Pictorials Ltd p 7 left; Public
Records Office, London p 24.

The publishers have made every effort to trace the
copyright holders, but if they have inadvertently
overlooked any, they will be pleased to make the necessary
arrangements at the earliest opportunity.

PREFACE

The study of history is exciting, whether in a good story well told, a mystery solved by the judicious unravelling of clues, or a study of the men, women and children whose fears and ambitions, successes and tragedies make up the collective memory of mankind.

This series aims to reveal this excitement to pupils through a set of topic books on important historical subjects from the Middle Ages to the present day. Each book contains four main elements: a narrative and descriptive text, lively and relevant illustrations, extracts of contemporary evidence, and questions for further thought and work. Involvement in these elements should provide an adventure which will bring the past to life in the imagination of the pupil.

Each book is also designed to develop the knowledge, skills and concepts so essential to a pupil's growth. It provides a wide, varying introduction to the evidence available on each topic. In handling this evidence, pupils will increase their understanding of basic historical concepts such as causation and change, as well as of more advanced ideas such as revolution and democracy. In addition, their use of basic study skills will be complemented by more sophisticated historical skills such as the detection of bias and the formulation of opinion.

The intended audience for the series is pupils of eleven to sixteen years: it is expected that the earlier topics will be introduced in the first three years of secondary school, while the nineteenth and twentieth century topics are directed towards first examinations.

INTRODUCTION

In April, 1536, at the end of the twenty-seventh year of the reign of King Henry VIII, there were, scattered through England and Wales, more than 800 religious houses, monasteries, nunneries and friaries and in them lived close on 10 000 monks, canons, nuns and friars. Four years later, in April 1540, there were none.

G.W.O. Woodward: *Dissolution of the Monasteries*, 1972

All that remained, with few exceptions, were abandoned buildings which were robbed of their stone or which were left to crumble. The ruins of these monasteries are still with us today. If you have visited one you will know what a ghostly place it can be. Roofless walls of bare stone stand chill, damp and shadowy. Here a pointed window where once stained glass could be seen and there a jutting stone which once supported the wooden beams of the roof. On the ground below, some tiles and metal studs are the only remains of the effigy of some great abbot. As you walk from building to building, you follow the footsteps of the monks who, more than four centuries before, would have been going about their daily business. In your imagination you can easily confuse the moving shadows and muffled footsteps of a fellow visitor with the wanderings of a monk haunting the house from which he was ejected all those years ago. Why were the monasteries destroyed? How much did they fight for survival? What became of the monks, their buildings and their land? These are the questions which will be posed in the following chapters.

Rievaulx Abbey, Yorkshire

A NEW REIGN BEGINS

The new monk

services: there were usually
three services before dawn,
three more during the day,
one at sunset and one just
before bedtime

The bell of Cartmel Priory tolled at 2 a.m. to wake the monks and call them to the first service of the day. A young monk rubbed his eyes, dressed and made his way down the night stairs. He crossed the nave and went into the choir where the service would be held. A life of devotion to God could be harsh, and the early service was the most demanding part of all – but once matins was over, he returned to bed until dawn and the call of the second service. After this his routine took him to the cloister, where he washed his face and hands in the lavatorium before taking breakfast in the refectory. Until he re-entered the cloister he spoke to nobody – conversation was forbidden at mealtimes, when the only voice to be heard was that of a monk standing in a wall pulpit reading lessons from the Bible.

The nave at Fountains Abbey, Yorkshire

The cloister was normally a place for meditation, for reading, and for copying pages from the Bible. Now, however, the young monk was able to snatch a few words of conversation with his fellows before the daily meeting in the chapter house. This was the time and place for day to day business: accounts were prepared, work schedules were made, and occasionally monks were punished. This particular day was different. Important news had arrived at remote Cartmel, a small priory at the foot of the Lake District, over 300 km from London. King Henry VII was dead, and a new king, Henry VIII, had come to the throne. The prior read a letter to the assembled company – a letter of congratulation which he had written from the priory to the new king. The letter was also a pledge of loyalty, and a wish for the King's favour during a long and happy reign.

The rest of the day passed as usual for the young monk. There were six more services; he spent some time helping the cellarer unload barrels and he assisted the almoner in the handing out of gifts of bread to the local poor. He also had a rare chance to show some travelling merchants around – they had admired the guest house, but

Below left: *Note the wall pulpit on the right*
Below right: *The chapter house at Worcester Cathedral*

oddly they spoke most highly of the reredorter, which they said made life far cleaner than throwing human waste into the streets. Later he went to the kitchen to fetch some food for an aged monk in the infirmary. But most of all, like other days, this was a day of prayer and thought. One thought which certainly did not enter the young monk's head was this: that the same king for whom he had just offered special prayers would bring about the downfall of Cartmel Priory and the death of the monks who sought to defend it; and worse, that within 30 years Henry VIII would close all of the monasteries and priories in this fair land.

Using the evidence

Look at the plan of a typical monastery. In the boxes surrounding the plan are clues to the purpose of each building: sketches, and references to pages where pictures of those buildings can be found. Draw your own version of the plan. Use a double page and leave room for the boxes. Then in the boxes, name each part of the monastery. Use the account you have just read to describe what each building was used for. If there is still room in the box, draw your own sketch.

If you are able to visit a local monastery, use a more accurate plan of your own.

The new king

When Henry VIII came to the throne in 1509 he was a delight to his subjects. His father, Henry VII, had been an efficient but very dull king. Although his court had been splendid, most people only remembered that they had paid him a great deal of money and had not seen much for it. Indeed, he shunned glory and war, and saved as much as possible so that when he died, his son, Henry VIII, inherited a considerable fortune in money, plate and jewels.

The new king was a complete contrast to his father. He dazzled his people and foreigners alike:

> *His majesty is the handsomest potentate I ever set eyes on: above the usual height, with an extremely fine calf to his leg, his complexion fair and bright, with auburn hair combed short and a face so round and beautiful that it would become a pretty woman.*

State papers

Above: *Henry VII and Henry VIII. A father and son with little in common*

Right: *The young Henry VIII. You may like to draw your own version, and use the description of Henry to add the detail and colour*

He was extremely talented. As a young king he spent his time:

> *exercising himself daily in shooting, singing, dancing, wrestling, casting at the bar, playing recorders, flutes, virginals and in setting of songs.*

State papers

virginals and music: England was a centre of musical composition in Tudor times. Henry prided himself on his ability to write music. The virginal was an instrument like a piano, but lighter and sharper in sound

He was also very extravagant. In fashion, he led the way with magnificent clothing and jewellery. In 1515 the Venetian ambassador described the King's clothing:

> *he wore a cap of crimson velvet . . . with gold enamelled tags. His doublet was striped with white and crimson satin. Very close round his neck he had a gold collar, from which there hung a round cut diamond the size of the largest walnut I ever saw, and to this was suspended a most beautiful and very round pearl. His mantle was purple velvet lined with white satin.*

Venetian papers

Fifteen years later Henry's partiality for clothes and fine jewels had not diminished. The following payments were made for the King's expenses in December 1530:

Paid to a clockmaker for eleven clocks	£19 16s. 8d.
Paid to James Hobart as a reward for bringing sweet oranges and lemons	£1 0s. 0d.
Paid for five falcons	£7 6s. 8d.
Paid to a poor man that had 13 children	£3 6s. 8d.
Paid to John Baptist the Italian jeweller for certain jewels	£295 3s. 4d.
Paid to my lady Anne in groats for playing money	£20 0s. 0d.
Paid to Alart Plymmer the jeweller for certain jewels	£1731 6s. 8d.
Paid to John Baptist for pearls	£373 9s. 3d.
Paid to the King for playing money 200 crowns worth	£46 13s. 3d.
Paid to Laurence Lee, one of the Keepers of the King's Hounds for a month's wage	9s. 0d.

N.H. Nicholas: *Expenses of Henry VIII*, 1827

money: accounts in the sixteenth century were usually written in Roman numerals. They mainly used pounds, shillings and pence, as in this account, but other coins included marks (13s. 4d.) and groats ($\frac{1}{4}$d.) as well as crowns

---

Questions

Look at the list of expenses.

1 What evidence is there to show that the King enjoyed hunting and gambling?

2 The total expenses for this month (some payments having been omitted) were £4464 16s. 9d. Approximately what proportion of that was spent on jewels and pearls?

Hampton Court. This wonderful palace, close to the River Thames, was built by Cardinal Wolsey. It outshone the King's own palaces, and it seems that Henry VIII wanted it for himself. The use of brick, the windows, chimneys, and dark panelled rooms are all typical of the age. Here we see the clock, which was added to the palace by Henry. Can you see what it tells as well as the time?

3   The amount spent on pearls and jewels is over 5 000 times Laurence Lee's wages. If you take an average monthly wage now and multiply by 5 000, what would be the value of the pearls and jewels today?

Henry also entertained on a lavish scale. Consider the preparations which he made for visiting guests:

> *Then the King brought the Ambassador to the new banquet chamber, which was hanged with a costly verdor all new, the ground thereof was all gold and the flowers were all of satin silver. Then the King, Queen and ambassadors sat down to supper and were served with 90 dishes.*
>
> E. Hall: *The Triumphant Reign of King Henry VIII*, 1904

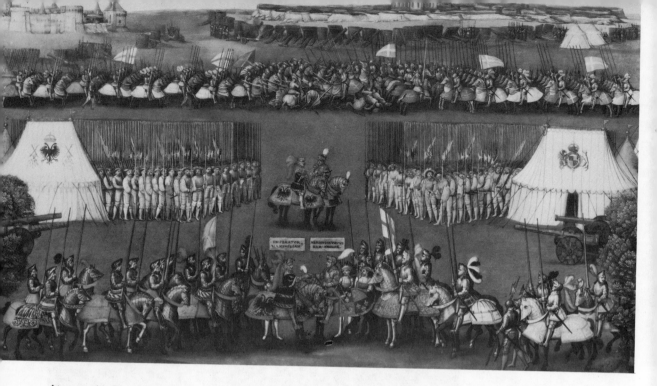

A far more extraordinary and extravagant spectacle was the meeting in 1520 between Henry and Francis I of France. This occasion is remembered as the meeting at the Field of the Cloth of Gold. It was first of all a diplomatic meeting, and may have been intended to keep peace between England and France. However, the two countries had been enemies for a long time, and their kings were both young, proud and ambitious. This was an occasion when they were determined to impress, and no money was spared in the tremendous preparations for the meeting.

Francis I: Henry and Francis had much in common – youth, power, love of sport and vanity. So they were bound to be rivals, and wished to defeat each other in the greatest combat – war

A castle at Guisnes, near Calais (then under English control), was converted, and a large camp was added to it, to accommodate the five thousand people who would follow their king to France. Part of the camp was a summer palace, built of cloth on a brick foundation:

> *The walls rising above the brickwork to a height of about thirty feet were of painted cloth mounted on timber frames. They were set with glass windows. The sloping roof was painted to resemble slates. A mighty gateway gave entrance to the palace, while outside this arch were two fountains.... eyewitnesses say that wine ran from them incessantly.*
>
> S. Anglo: *Spectacle, Pageantry and Early Tudor Policy*, 1969

Long lists can still be seen showing the quantity of food taken across the English Channel. The amount of meat and fish is staggering:

373	oxen		9 100	plaice
2 014	muttons		700	conger eels
842	veal		5 554	soles

The Field of the Cloth of Gold. What is happening in the picture? Compare it with the description on this and the opposite page, and use this information to help you with the exercise on page 14

Some of the other ingredients are suprising:

2	sturgeons	92	cygnets	86	bitterns
1	dolphin	313	herons	2	peacocks
3	porpoises	76	storks	11	egrets

And it is hard to imagine:

67 370 eggs   *432.5 gallons of cream*   *98 tuns of wine*
State papers

The fleet and its provisions were made ready at Dover, and in June 1520 they crossed to France where the 8000 workmen had now finished the camp.

On 7 June the two kings met. Each of them, backed by their company, took up position on raised ground on opposite sides of the Field of the Cloth of Gold (the hill on one side had been altered so that neither king was above the other). It was almost like the meeting of two great armies until the trumpets sounded and:

> *Both Kings spurred their horses, galloped forward to the agreed point – marked by a spear stuck in the ground – and embraced two or three times, still in the saddle and bonnets in hand.*
>
> J.J. Scarisbrick: *Henry VIII*, 1968

There followed a fortnight of sport, feasting and entertainment. For a short time it seemed that there would be peace between England and France, but within a few weeks of Henry's return to England he turned against the French and made a treaty with Spain. The Field of the Cloth of Gold, whether a charade or a genuine attempt at peace, had been little more than a vastly extravagant show.

Henry jousting

13

War

Henry was not satisfied with magnificent display. The sport of kings was war, and despite diplomatic shows such as the Field of the Cloth of Gold, Henry always had an ambition to fight the French. Indeed, when the French ambassadors came to congratulate Henry at his coronation he insulted them. He also laid claim to the throne of France, a claim which was now a century out of date.

However, England was poorly equipped to fight a war. In normal times Henry had an army of only 200 soldiers. It was the custom that in time of war kings would raise more troops, but it must have come as a surprise to many Englishmen when Henry announced that he wanted a huge force of 30 000. An army of such size would have cost a fortune in wages alone, but Henry also wanted it to be the best equipped and most impressive army in Europe. The Venetian ambassador wrote:

> *These English go a good pace I can tell you . . . and enormous preparations are being made . . . night and day and all festivals the cannon founders are at work.*

Venetian papers

Tudor cannon. Although a relatively new invention, these cannons could fire over a mile

The tower armoury: in the White Tower at the Tower of London, there are several suits of armour which belonged to Henry VIII. Try to see them, and you will become aware of the true glory of this king

galeas: a ship powered by both oar and sail

At this time the art of gunnery was expanding, and Henry ordered 12 cannon which, by the standards of the day, were massive. England did not have good armourers, so he ordered armour from Italy and Spain and encouraged Italian craftsmen to come and settle in England. Some of Henry's magnificent suits of armour were made by these Italians at Greenwich.

Henry also wanted ships. The greatest of these was the *Henry Grace de Dieu*, or *Great Harry*. This vast ship which cost £7 708 was described by the Venetians as:

> *A galeas of unusual magnitude with such a number of heavy guns that their weight would be too much for the strongest castle. It appears to be a very fine craft, provided it can be worked.*
>
> Venetian papers

The launching of the ship was conducted with Henry's usual flair:

> *The King was dressed galley fashion, with a vest of gold brocade reaching to the middle of the thigh, breeches of cloth of gold and scarlet hose, a gold chain more than four fingers breadth, a gold whistle more than a span in length, and a number of jewels on either side.*
>
> Venetian papers

The Great Harry

Henry's wars

Date	Reason for war	Cost	Taxes received	Details of the war
1512–15	War with France and her ally Scotland, to claim the throne of France	£900 000	£320 000	The army which crossed into France in 1512 was 'demoralised by drink and ruined by disease'. In 1513 the army surprised a French cavalry force, which turned and ran with some losses. 'Henry was well in the rear, leading his regiments from behind.' Henry captured two towns but 'the expedition was a futile side-show' with almost no effect on the war. Henry had proved his incompetence and came as near to being a figure of fun as he ever was to do
1522–5	War had been renewed between France and Spain. Henry hoped to gain from this and claimed the French throne again	£400 000	£210 000 then a forced loan which caused widespread rioting	The main expedition of 1523 was intended to attack Paris and join with the Spaniards there. That plan failed through poor supply. Instead an attack was made on Boulogne, which failed through poor weapons. Meanwhile the French king was heavily defeated by the Spanish, and England was not given any share of the victory. 'Too short of money to raise an army, Henry had little alternative but to make peace'
1542	England and Spain again went to war with Scotland and France. Henry's motive was 'largely self-glorification, a desire to relive in late middle age the triumphs of youth'	£1 300 000 + cost of coastal defence	£650 000 + loans and sales of Crown lands worth £600 000	Scotland was savagely subdued in the first campaign. Then 48 000 troops crossed to France, but instead of attacking Paris Henry captured Boulogne. The French counter-attacked and a fleet reached Portsmouth. This was the occasion of the sinking of the *Mary Rose*, in itself a humiliation for the King. Finally Henry was paid to release Boulogne but 'it was a hollow victory'. The whole war was an expensive fiasco

Mary Rose: the sinking of the now famous *Mary Rose* was a disaster for Henry, but has provided a treasure trove for modern archaeologists and historians. A museum of the *Mary Rose* can now be visited at Portsmouth

Thomas Wolsey. In his early years as king, Henry relied mostly upon Wolsey to govern the country. He became Chancellor of England, Archbishop of York and held many other offices in addition. He began the building of Hampton Court which was a clear sign of his status and wealth

Needless to say, all this was very expensive. In peacetime English kings were expected to live on their own income, without taxing the people. Henry VII had managed to save money by efficient collection of his income and by spending little. Henry VIII was not so efficient, and as we have seen was very extravagant. Preparations for war quickly used up his inheritance from Henry VII. An entry in Cardinal Wolsey's notebook shows that he was worried about the future:

Things to be remembered by the King's Grace touching his going in person with one army into France: First how money is to be got to the extent of £640 000 per year.

State papers

As can be seen in the table entitled 'Henry's wars', one of the ways was to increase taxes – and at first the people did not complain. However, there was widespread rioting in the 1520s, and Henry could not risk losing support during the break with Rome (see page 18) by asking for heavy taxes. Throughout the middle part of his reign Henry was forced to manage on less than he needed. However, he continued to be very extravagant and his wars used massive sums of money.

Questions

Look at the table entitled *Henry's wars*.

1 How much greater is expenditure in war than receipts from taxation?
2 How necessary do these wars seem to have been? Did the taxpayers get their money's-worth?

Where would he get the extra money? There were some who said that it should come from the Church. These people, who hated the wealth and power of the Church, were called anticlerical. A typical anticlerical view written by Simon Fish was that bishops and abbots:

had gotten into their hands more than a third part of all your realm. . . . and what do these greedy sort of sturdy idle holy thieves do? Truly nothing saving seducing wives. Are they not stronger in your own parliament house than yourself?

English Historical Documents, vol. V

Before 1529 not many people would have thought seriously of the king solving his financial problems by taking the money and property of the Church. Some small monasteries had been closed recently, but only because they were in decay. Most monasteries were still strong and had great influence.

Then, in 1529, a series of important events occurred which were to give Henry a reason to attack the Church.

THE BREAK WITH ROME

Martin Luther: Luther was one of the most important people of his time. He was a priest who criticised the pope and various aspects of Catholic ceremony and belief. He was a major influence in Europe's struggle with the Catholic church and became the leader of the German Reformation

Catherine of Aragon. She is usually thought of as old and dull, but remember that she and Henry began his reign young and happy

For centuries England, like the rest of Europe, had been a loyal Catholic country, with the pope in Rome as head of the Church. When Henry VIII came to the throne there was no reason to believe that this would change, because the new king was deeply religious. The Venetian ambassador wrote that the King 'heard three masses daily when he hunted, and sometimes five on other days'.

Henry was proud of his religious knowledge, and the Pope had given him the title 'Defender of the Faith', for writing a book which defended the Pope against the criticism of a German reformer called Martin Luther. However, Henry did not stay in the Pope's favour for long; they had a quarrel which was to bring dramatic changes in England's religion. The cause of this quarrel was the problem of Henry's marriage. For 17 years Henry had been contentedly married to his Spanish queen, Catherine of Aragon. Then, in 1527, he asked the Pope to free him from the marriage so that he could marry again.

What brought about this desire for a new wife? Historians have put forward various reasons:

A *Good wife though she was, Catherine of Aragon had failed in her primary function, to provide Henry with a healthy male heir. It had not been for lack of trying. She had borne her first baby in January 1510. It had been a daughter, still-born. Within a year she produced a son .... but then the child had sickened and died. 1513 saw the birth of another boy, and 1514 yet another, but neither survived. In the same year Catherine was delivered prematurely of a fourth son,*

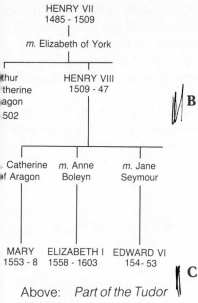

HENRY VII
1485 - 1509
|
m. Elizabeth of York
|

thur   HENRY VIII
therine   1509 - 47
agon
502

Catherine   m. Anne   m. Jane
of Aragon   Boleyn   Seymour

MARY   ELIZABETH I   EDWARD VI
1553 - 8   1558 - 1603   154- 53

Above: *Part of the Tudor
family tree*
Below: *Anne Boleyn.
Some thought that she had
bewitched the King*

the pope: in the sixteenth century the pope was more than head of the Catholic church, he was also head of the Papal states, which frequently became involved in politics and wars. This explains why Pope Clement VII was so easily influenced by a foreign power such as Spain

still-born. Not until 1516 did she produce a sturdy living child, and then it was a girl, christened Mary. There were several more pregnancies, but no son came, and before long Catherine's pregnancies ceased.

Robert Lacy: *The Life and Times of King Henry VIII*, 1972

B Catherine had first been married to Henry's eldest brother, Arthur, who had died at the age of 14. Henry had then married his brother's widow, and only later was he troubled by passages in the Bible which said:

And if a man shall take his brother's wife, it is an unclean thing ... they shall be childless. I set before you this day a blessing and a curse; A blessing if ye obey the commandments of the Lord your God, and a curse if ye will not obey.

Leviticus, XVIII

C *The King had tired of his wife and fallen in love with Anne Boleyn, who would give herself entirely to him only if he would give himself entirely to her.*

J.J. Scarisbrick: *Henry VIII*, 1968

Using the evidence
Henry is preparing his case to justify his divorce from Catherine of Aragon. Which of the above reasons does he use when writing to each of the following:
a) the Pope
b) a close friend
c) parliament.
Explain your choice in each case.

In normal circumstances the divorce would have been granted, even though this was a most unusual case. However, these were not normal circumstances. By a most unfortunate coincidence, Catherine of Aragon's nephew, Charles V of Spain, had captured Rome in 1527 and was in control of Pope Clement VII. Whether or not the Pope sympathised with Henry's case, Charles would not allow his aunt to be put aside by the English king.

Henry and Cardinal Wolsey tried in various ways to change the Pope's mind. When they failed Wolsey was made scapegoat and sacked. But the answer to the problem was provided by Henry's new minister, Thomas Cromwell. Cromwell saw that the Pope would never give way, and that a more drastic answer was needed – to break away from Rome and make Henry head of his own Church in England. This was a very difficult task, but Cromwell found that he had some important friends who would help him. In particular there were many

Key Acts of the Reformation: firstly, payments of money to Rome were stopped by the Acts of Annates. Then the Pope's right to make judgments (such as whether or not Henry could marry Anne) was stopped by the Act of Restraint of Appeals. Finally the Act of Supremacy made the king Head of the Church

men in parliament who agreed with the new ideas of Martin Luther, and there where those such as Simon Fish who did not like the wealth and power of the Church. Cromwell was able to make use of this ill-feeling in parliament to push through a series of acts which brought the Church under the King's control and thus severed all links with Rome.

This had two immediate effects: firstly, Henry became 'Supreme Head of the Church of England'; and secondly, he was able to arrange his own divorce, and subsequently to marry Anne Boleyn.

Using the evidence
Make a copy of the flow diagram and complete it to show the progress of the divorce.

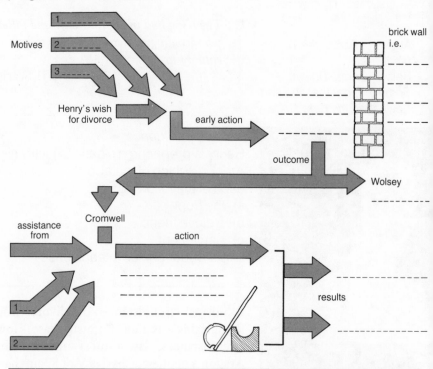

The King had got what he wanted, but would the people agree to the changes? To make sure that they did, everyone was forced to take the Oath of Supremacy, a pledge of loyalty to their king as head of the Church.

Only a small number of people refused to take the oath. The most famous of these was Sir Thomas More, who was tried and executed. The greatest opposition in numbers came from the monks. Eighteen monks of the Carthusian and Bridgettine orders suffered terrible deaths because they would not go along with the King. For example, three of them, John Houghton, Robert Lawrence and Augustine

Thomas Cromwell. Cromwell was the administrative genius who solved the problem of the King's divorce, and reformed his government. He is the person most associated with the closure of the monasteries

order of monks: there were several different types (or orders) of monks and nuns, and they lived according to differing rules. The larger orders included the Augustinians and the Cistercians. Smaller orders such as the Carthusians and the Bridgettines were the strictest. Carthusian monks lived in separate cells, not dormitories, and they rarely spoke

Webster, who were all priors in the Carthusian order of monks, were executed at Tyburn, London, in May 1534. Their execution was described by an eyewitness:

They were hanged, cut down alive, drawn to another place, put on their feet, stripped of their clothes, disembowelled, and had their bowels burnt before their eyes while they yet breathed ... They certainly would not have suffered such barbarities to the Turk.

State papers

This was a particularly cruel death because the executioner did not even allow them to be put out of their misery before disembowelling, as was usual. A modern novelist has no doubt who was responsible for

Hanging, drawing and quartering

this cruelty, as she shows in this conversation between Henry VIII and Sir Henry Norris, who reported on the execution:

> 'And they lived yet when they were cut down?'
> 'One of them lived till both arms were off. But all while they were opened and drawn.'
> The King bowed his head.
> 'The executioner did his work with a will?' he asked.
> 'With a will. He rubbed their very hearts, hot and steaming over their mouths.'
> 'Did they cry for mercy?' he asked suddenly. Norris said that they did. It was a lie, but the King nodded as if pleased and that was what Norris cared for.
>
> H.F.M. Prescott: *Man on a Donkey*, 1953

For the time being the other monks took the Oath of Supremacy. The monks of Burgh St Peter were typical. They wrote:

> We ... and our successors will always display fidelity [loyalty] regard and obedience towards our Lord Henry VIII and towards Queen Anne his wife and towards his offspring. Also that we always will hold that the aforesaid King is head of the Church of England.
>
> *English Historical Documents*, vol. V

Despite this, Henry may not have trusted the monks. Their life was totally devoted to religion, so they had the most to lose by any changes. Also, they could be a dangerous centre of opposition if any Catholics wanted to rebel against the King. For Henry, England would be a safer place without monks. This danger, and Henry's financial needs, gave the King two strong motives to begin the dissolution (or closure) of the monasteries.

Using the evidence

Which of these statements do you believe to be true, and which false? Give reasons from the above text to justify your answer.

1 a) The monks supported the King because he had a strong case, and the Pope should have given him a divorce.
   b) The monks took the Oath of Supremacy out of fear.
   c) The monks took the oath because changes in the law were made by parliament, and parliament represented the people.
   Could there be any other reasons?

2 In the light of your answer to question 1, did the King have anything to fear from the monks?

THE MONASTERIES

The condition of the monasteries

The decision to close some of the monasteries was made during the quarrel with the Pope. As early as 1532 the Spanish ambassador, Eustace Chapuys, believed that Henry was 'determined to reunite to the crown the goods which churchman held of it'.

Two years later Chapuys reported that Thomas Cromwell had said that he 'would make his master more wealthy than all the other Princes of Christendom'. By this time the break with Rome was nearly complete. Several Acts of Parliament had been passed to cut off the Pope's power in England. One of these Acts stated that all payments which had been made to the pope should now be made to the king. Cromwell wanted to find out exactly how much the King should be getting, so he sent out commissioners to make a survey. Their reports were put into a great book called the *Valor Ecclesiasticus*. This contained details of:

This comes from the front page of the Valor Ecclesiasticus. *What is its main feature? Why not start one of your pages like this?*

The number and names of every abbey, monastery priory and the names of all the manors, lands tenements, rents and possessions belonging to every abbey and their whole yearly value.
Valor Ecclesiasticus Tempore Henrici Octavus Institus, 1825 ed.

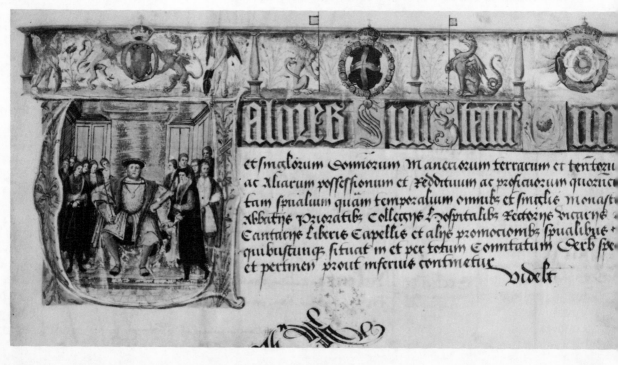

It has been suggested that the results of this survey convinced Cromwell that the monasteries were the answer to Henry's money problems. By closing only the weakest he could bring into Henry's hands lands worth £40 000 per year.

Cromwell knew that there were many people who valued the monasteries and who would defend them. To close the monasteries just because Henry needed the money was bound to cause opposition, and as most monks had taken the Oath of Supremacy he could not say that they opposed the King. Another reason for closure had to be found.

To provide this excuse, another commission was sent out. The two men in charge, Richard Layton and Thomas Legh, visited every monastery and reported on the conduct of the monks. The outcome was a book called the *Compendium Compertorium* (1535), which showed the monasteries to be in a dreadful state. As a result of the report, the government was able to justify closing the smaller monasteries, those worth under £200 (some 600 out of the 800 monasteries in England).

What evidence did Layton and Legh find against the monasteries? Here are some examples:

Layton and Legh: these were the men mainly responsible for the survey of the monasteries. They were very efficient, but have been accused of dishonesty. Those who opposed the attack on monasteries regarded these two men as their main enemy

Fountains Abbey in Yorkshire

The abbot has so greatly dilapidated his house, wasted their woods, notoriously keeping six women. He committed theft and sacrilege. At midnight he caused his chaplain to steal the sexton's keys, and took out a jewel and a cross of gold with stones. He sold them to one Warren, a goldsmith.

The cellarium and lay-brothers' refectory at Fountains Abbey, Yorkshire

Christchurch, Canterbury

The prior ... wrote an inventory of jewels and plate belonging to the monastery, with certain items of silver, gold and stone to the value of thousands of pounds wilfully left out. His monks shall never give evidence in this matter because they fear that they should be poisoned or murdered in prison, as the common report is that he has murdered several others.

Farley, Wiltshire

The prior has only eight women, and the rest of the monks fewer.

Shulbrede, Sussex

The prior has seven [women] and his monks four or five each.

Pentney Priory, Norfolk

The Prior has broken his vow of chastity, as appears from the confession of the abbess of Marham.

Langdon Priory, Kent
The abbot's house joined fields and wood, and was like a cony clapper [rabbit warren], full of starting holes [bolt holes]. I stood a great space knocking at the abbot's door. I found a short poleaxe and with it I dashed the abbot's door in pieces. And about the house I go with the poleaxe in my hand, for the abbot is a dangerous knave and a hardy. But for a conclusion his whore, alias his gentlewoman, bestirred her stumps towards the starting holes, and there Bartlett took the tender damsel. I found her clothes in the abbot's coffer.

State papers

Using evidence such as this, it was easy for the government to make out a strong case that the monasteries were no longer fulfilling their purpose, and should be closed down.

Using the evidence

Were the monasteries as bad as Layton and Legh said? There are two ways in which we can check the truth of the report. Firstly, we can look for faults in the evidence itself. Secondly, we can compare it with other available evidence.

A   Questioning the evidence itself
Is there any reason to criticise the reports of Layton and Legh? For example:
a) are the accusations detailed?
b) is any of their evidence based on hearsay rather than proof?
c) is there any evidence of exaggeration or sarcasm?
Why are a, b, and c important points to consider when looking at the evidence?

B   Comparison with other sources
Two other types of evidence about the monasteries can be found. Firstly, from time to time bishops visited monasteries to inspect them. Often reports revealed no faults, but if any rules were found to be broken the bishops stated a suitable punishment. The reports of their visits, which were confidential, make a very useful comparison with the government report.

Secondly, there is further evidence in the form of reports made at the time of closure. Of course, by this time the fate of the monastery had been decided. These reports were also confidential, and were sent to the King's Principal Secretary, Thomas Cromwell.

Evidence from the bishops' inspections:

Ramsey Priory, visited in 1517
The Prior is a bad tempered drunkard, easy with his friends and severe to brutality with others. The senior monks, having

sent the juniors to office (prayers) went off to dice for money, accompanying their gaming with hideous oaths.

St Frideswide's Abbey, Oxford, visited in 1517 and 1520
One monk was disobedient, and no grammar master was kept. Six monks were absent, and no accounts were kept.

Leicester Abbey, visited in 1527
When the abbot did attend choir, he took with him his fool, who caused distraction and laughter with his sallies and snatches of song.

Dorchester Abbey, visited in 1530
The monks went out to fish and hunt, and only attended choir three times a year.

Missenden Abbey, Buckinghamshire, visited in 1530
The buildings were in disrepair. The abbot and a monk had been guilty of repeated misconduct with the wife of a villager.

Evidence of the commissioners for closure, 1536–7

Farley Priory, Wiltshire
There are six monks, all of honest lifestyle.

Pentney Priory, Norfolk
It would be a pity not to spare a house that feeds so many poor, which is in a good state, maintains good service, and does so many charitable deeds.

Rievaulx Abbey, Yorkshire

D. Knowles: *Religious Orders in England*, vol. III, 1959

1 Divide your page into two columns.
  In the left hand column list the types of crime which appear in
  the government report made by Layton and Legh and the
  number of examples of that crime cited.
  In the right hand column list the types of accusation made by
  the bishops, and the number of examples cited.
2 Compare directly the evidence of Layton and Legh with that of
  the commissioners, concerning Farley and Pentney.
3 How do you explain the differences between the two sets of
  reports?
4 In your opinion, were the monasteries in such bad condition
  that they deserved closure, or can you suggest alternative
  remedies?

You may have decided, as many historians have, that the government's case against the monasteries was only an excuse for closure. The report of 1535–6 made the monasteries seem far worse than they actually were. Indeed, the evidence we have seen here is amongst the most damning, and many monasteries were not guilty of any crimes. To summarise, there can be little doubt that the monasteries did not deserve to be closed for the reasons given. Greed and fear were the real motives for closure.

Using the evidence
Draw your own version of the cartoon and complete it to show the
real and the given reasons for closing the monasteries.

The closure of the smaller monasteries

There can be little doubt that the government had made its decision to close the monasteries before they had received the report of Layton and Legh in 1535–6. We have already seen the details of the report, which must have been made to justify the closure. As a result an Act of Parliament was passed in 1536 which stated that:

> *for as much as manifest sin, vicious carnal and abominable living is daily used and committed among the little and small abbeys and priories, whereby they spoil, destroy, consume and utterly waste their churches, monasteries and priories . . . unless such houses be utterly suppressed there can be no reformation in this behalf.*
> *[Therefore] His Majesty will have and enjoy such monasteries which have not in lands above the clear yearly value of £200.*
>
> Parliamentary statutes

Monks who wished to continue in their holy order were to be transferred to the 'divers and great solemn monasteries where, thanks be to God, religion is right well kept and observed.'

Almost immediately the process of closure began. Commissioners were sent out to visit the 600 smaller monasteries and to show them a copy of the Act. They then had to send back to London answers to a set of questions. Here are the questions, and the response of one priory in Leicestershire:

Q *What is the name of the Priory?*
A *The Priory of Ulverscroft.*
Q *What is the order of religion here?*
A *They are Black canons of the rule of St. Austen. It stands in a wilderness in Charnewood Forest, and refreshes many poor and wayfaring people.*
Q *What is the yearly value of the house?*
A *£85 0s 11d.*
Q *What number of persons of religion be there, and the conduct of their lives, and how many of them will go to other houses of religion and how many will take capacities [a payment made to them if they leave their holy order]?*
A *Eight beside the prior, a wise discreet man; six are priests, good, virtuous, religious and of good qualities as writers, embroiderers and painters. They desire the King to establish them there [allow them to continue] or otherwise to set them over to some other house of the same religion. Other persons having their living of the house include 20 yeomen, 14 children for the chapel, 3 women for the dairy . . .*
Q *What is the value of the bells and lead?*
A *The bells and lead are worth £108 5s $\frac{1}{2}$d., are in good repair, and much has been built here within the last three years.*

Q *What is the value of ornaments, plate, jewels, chattels, ready money, household stuff, corn, stock and store?*
A *£137 17s 2d.*
Q *What is the value of the land of the priory?*
A *There are 449 acres of woods, park and forest worth £745.*

State papers

Having made the survey the commissioner was given instructions to take possession of the abbey seal, and any charters and other important documents. If there was no chance that the monastery could be saved, the monks were sent away, either to a larger monastery, or to seek other work. Some monasteries escaped closure, either because they made a strong appeal, or because there was no room in a large house of the same order for the monks who wished to continue in holy orders. Gradually, the rest were closed. But before they had all been visited, the government faced its first great opposition.

Questions

1 Do you think that, at this stage, the government intended to close all the monasteries?
2 Why do you think that the commissioners were asked to value the moveable goods, the lead and bells, and the land separately?
3 Make out a case to justify the continued existence of Ulverscroft Priory.

Battle Abbey, Sussex

Resistance

Few of the monks in the smaller monasteries were willing to use force to defend their houses, and risk the dreadful punishments suffered by the Carthusians in 1534 (see page 20). But, it was not always easy for the commissioners:

The King's Commissioners in Cheshire were lately at Norton to suppress the Abbey. They had packed up the jewels and stuff and were parting on the morrow when the Abbot gathered a company of 200 or 300 persons, and the Commissioners were forced to take to the tower. Divers fires were lit within and without the gates. The Abbot had caused an ox and other victuals to be killed for his company.

State papers

Whitby Abbey, Yorkshire

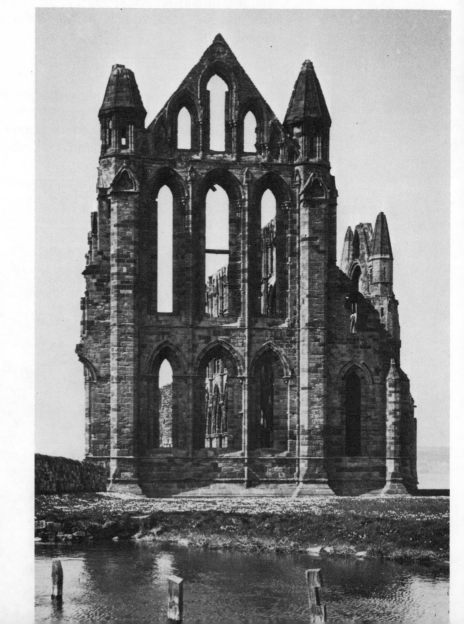

Early on the following morning the sheriff arrived and drove away most of the defenders, and the abbot was arrested and taken to Chester Castle.

At Exeter, while the commissioners were at dinner, one of their workman was alone in the priory when:

> *certain women came in all haste to the said church, some with spikes, some with shovels, and some with such tools as they could get and, the church door being fast, they broke it open. And finding the man there pulling down the rood loft they hurled stones into him, in so much that for his safety he was driven to take to the tower. And yet they pursued him so eagerly that he was enforced to leap out at a window and so to save himself, and very hardly he escaped the breaking of his neck, and yet he brake one of his ribs.*
>
> *The Mayor came down with his officers, before whose coming they [the women] had made fast the church doors and had bestowed themselves in places to stand to their defences. Notwithstanding the mayor broke in upon them and with much ado he apprehended and took them all.*

State papers

At Hexham in Northumberland the commissioners did not even get into the priory. The prior announced that he and 20 armed monks within would 'die rather than surrender'. Later they paraded on the green with 60 armed supporters.

Before the disturbance at Hexham had been settled, a far greater challenge faced the government – a massive rebellion known as the Pilgrimage of Grace.

Questions
1 What similarities are there between the incidents at Norton and Exeter?
2 Why do you think there were so few cases where the monasteries defended themselves?

---

4 | THE PILGRIMAGE OF GRACE

On 1 October 1536 a small protest began in Lincolnshire which was to increase and to become the greatest threat to the rule of any Tudor monarch.

The protest began when a group of King's Commissioners arrived at the town of Louth to survey the monastery there. This caused a riot and news of this disturbance quickly spread, soon reaching the ears of a Yorkshireman called Robert Aske. He believed that the rebellion, which he called the Pilgrimage of Grace, was a crusade to defend the Church against recent changes. Robert Aske blamed all that he thought was wrong in England on:

> *evil disposed persons being of the King's Council who intend to destroy the Church of England and the ministers of the same. For this Pilgrimage we have taken it for the preservation of Christ's church of this realm of England, for the King our sovereign lord, the nobility and the commons of the same, for the reformation of that which is amiss within his realm, and for the punishment of heretics and such as be not worthy to remain near about the King our sovereign Lord's person.*

State papers

By 15 October, Aske and 20 000 rebels were outside the city of York, and others were flocking to join them from throughout the county. York surrendered to them without a fight, and Aske led a grand procession through the city. In the meantime the rebellion had spread to all of the northern counties, and only a handful of towns remained loyal to the King.

Aske's main aim was to gain complete control of the north, and to make every man swear the rebel oath. Another of his aims was to help the monks reopen the abbeys which had been closed, and naturally he expected help from the monks in monasteries great and small. In a statement which he wrote after the rebellion, Aske explained why he supported the monasteries:

> *The Abbeys in the north parts gave alms to poor men and laudably served God. The divine service is much diminished to the distress of the faith. No hospitality is now in those places kept. Also divers of the said abbeys were in the mountains and desert places where people be rude of condition and not well taught the law of God, and when the abbeys stood the people had not only worldly refreshing in their bodies but also spiritual information and preaching.*

Aske and Darcy: the two most important men in the rebellion. Robert Aske was a modest Yorkshire gentleman, training to be a lawyer. Lord Darcy was a nobleman, and his house at Pontefract Castle was a key centre of the rebellion

heretics: these were people who spoke against the existing laws and beliefs of the Church. This was regarded as a terrible crime, and many people were burned for heresy

Also the Abbeys were one of the beauties of this realm; gentlemen were much succoured in their needs with money, their young sons were educated and their daughters brought up in virtue; and such abbeys as were near the danger of sea banks were great maintainers of sea walls and dykes, maintainers and builders of bridges and highways and other such things.

State papers

The Pilgrimage of Grace

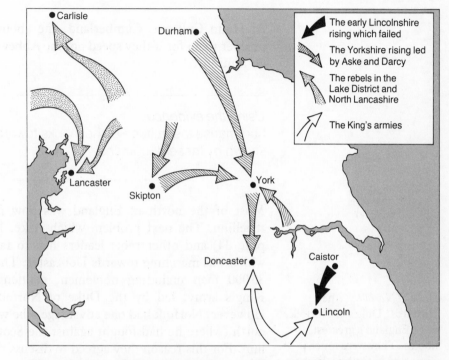

The response of the monasteries to Aske's call for help can be seen from the following documents.

At Sawley, Lancashire, a smaller house which had been suppressed, the monks were restored and the abbey became a centre of resistance. The monks there wrote the rebel marching song:

Alack Alack	*For there they had*
For the Churches Sake	*Both ale and bread*
Poor commons wake	*In time of need*
And no man marvel	*and succour great*
For clear it is	*In all distress*
The decay of this	*and Heaviness*
How the poor shall miss	*And well intreat.*
No tongue can tell	

State papers

At Jervaulx, a larger house in Yorkshire, the abbot:

conveyed himself by the back door to Witton Fell, where he tarried in a crag for four days.

At Furness, a larger house in Lancashire, the abbot urged the tenants to join the rising:

> *upon pain of death and pulling down their houses . . . Now must they stick together, for if they set down both you and the Holy Church is undone, for if they lack company we will go with them and live and die with them to defend their godly pilgrimage.*

State papers

At Holm Cultram, Cumberland, the abbot said: 'All Mighty God prosper them for if they speed not the Abbey is lost.' But he refused to go himself.

Using the evidence

Summarise the attitude of the monks towards the rebellion as shown by these documents.

Most of the north of England was now firmly in support of the rebellion. The next problem which Aske, Lord Darcy (see note on page 34) and other rebel leaders had to face was the King's army which was marching towards Doncaster. The rebel army consisted of 30 000 men including noblemen, gentlemen and commons. The King's army, led by the Duke of Norfolk, had only 8 000 men. However, Norfolk had one advantage – he was much respected in the north (where he had fought against the Scots) and the rebels trusted him. For this reason they agreed to discuss their complaints with him before taking any further action.

Duke of Norfolk: the Howards, Dukes of Norfolk, were England's greatest nobles. They were much respected in the North where the second Duke had led the English army into battle against the Scots in 1513

The rebels made many complaints, some of them having little to do with the monasteries. The problem which faces historians in their search for motives is to decide which of the complaints were really important. Even at the time of the Pilgrimage of Grace the Duke of Norfolk had difficulty in unscrambling the many grievances. This was especially so after the rebellion, when rebels told him their reasons for joining:

> *I came out of fear of loss of all my goods and I came forth for fear of burning of my house and defacing of my wife and children.*

State papers

Some idea of the rebels' motives can be gained from a study of their demands made to Norfolk:

1 To put an end to heresy
2 To return some powers to the Pope
3 To make Mary legitimate and heir to the throne
4 To restore the abbeys which had been closed

5 To punish Thomas Cromwell
6 To punish Layton and Legh
7 To make tenants more secure
8 To stop the enclosure of farmland
9 To be released from payment of taxes
10 To have a parliament in the north of England
11 To confirm privileges traditionally held by the Church
12 To repeal the treason acts
13 To have courts in the north as well as in London
14 To have a pardon

enclosure: the fencing (or enclosing) of fields was regarded as a great problem in Tudor times. In some areas people were thrown off their land and in others common land for grazing was greatly reduced. However bad, enclosure was disliked because it was new

---

Questions

1 How many of the rebel complaints can be related to anger at the closure of monasteries?
2 The complaints can be divided into three groups: religious; political/legal; social/economic. Copy out the diagram below. Group the motives under the three categories and write them into the spaces in the outer circle. Using a different colour for each category shade in the inner circle spaces and write the name of each category over its corresponding block of colour.

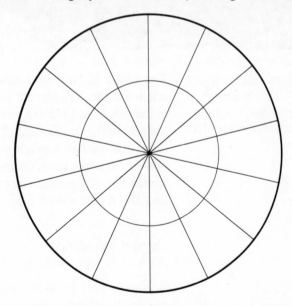

3 Are there any motives which are obviously those of poor rather than rich men, or those of the rich rather than the poor?
4 Can you make a general statement about the motives of the rebels?
5 Do you agree that the rebels would be glad to fight behind a banner of religion, even if they were not worried about changes in the Church. If so, why?

A nineteenth century view of the rebels. Do you agree that the artist had the right idea about the leader of the rising?

The Duke of Norfolk found himself in a very difficult position. On one hand the King wrote to him demanding the immediate dispersal of the rebels and the execution of ten ringleaders; evidently Henry did not realise the seriousness of the situation. On the other hand, Norfolk knew that he had a much weaker force than the rebels and was in no position to make them do anything. In order to get them to disperse he would have to make concessions. The only thing in his favour was that the rebels would also much rather negotiate than fight.

Using the evidence

In pairs, or as half the class, take the roles of Aske and Norfolk.

Rebels: decide secretly what is the least you will accept in answer to your demands before you agree to disperse. Put your demands into some order of priority ready for negotiation.

Norfolk: decide what is the maximum you can give to persuade the rebels to disperse, and remember that the King will be furious if you give away too much.

You must do everything possible to come to a peaceful solution. If you fail to do so, both sides will suffer.

In fact the outcome of the negotiations hardly mattered to the King. Norfolk had already written to him saying:

I beseech you to take in good part whatsoever promises I shall make unto the rebels, for surely I shall observe no part thereof for any respect of what others might call my honour.

State papers

So it was that Norfolk agreed to an unconditional pardon, a northern parliament and the return of monks to houses which had been closed. It was promised that all rebel complaints would be discussed at the northern parliament in York that the King himself would attend, and that he would even crown his new queen, Jane Seymour, there. Some monks did return to their houses – as was the case at Cartmel Priory in Cumberland.

Robert Aske was satisfied. On 8 December the rebels tore off their badges and swore loyalty to the King, saying:

We will all wear no badge nor sign but the badge of our Sovereign lord.

State papers

Henry VIII never intended to carry out any of his promises. Once the rebels had gone home the King's plan was to wait until their patience ran out. Any new rebellion would give him the excuse to break his promises and execute the ringleaders. In the meantime he called the rebel leaders to London, and kept up the pretence. Aske himself had an audience with the King, who gave him a handsome gown. The Spanish ambassador wrote a highly exaggerated account of the meeting to his master, Charles V of Spain:

'Be ye welcome my good Aske.' Henry was reported to have said 'It is my wish that here, before my council, you ask what you desire and I will grant it.' Aske answered 'Sire, your Majesty allows yourself to be governed by a tyrant named Cromwell. Everyone knows if it had not been for him 7 000 poor priests I have in my company would not be ruined wanderers as they are now.' Then the King, with a smiling face and words full of falseness, took from his neck a great chain of gold which he had put on for the purpose, and threw it round Aske's neck, saying to him 'I promise thee, thou art wiser than anyone thinks, and from this day forward I will make thee one of my council. Now return to the north and get your people to return to their houses'.

Spanish papers

Having won the confidence of the rebels, who were no doubt delighted to have challenged the King and escaped unpunished, Henry did nothing about his promises.

In January 1537, some gentlemen who distrusted the King attempted to revive the Pilgrimage of Grace, with an attack on the

Jane Seymour and Edward: Henry married Jane Seymour in 1536. This seems to have been a happy marriage, and at last in October 1537, Henry was given the son he so much wanted. Sadly, Jane never recovered from the birth and although her son, Edward VI, succeeded Henry he died young and without issue

Badge of five wounds worn by the rebels

loyal port of Hull. They failed dismally. Soon after, a second disturbance took place, this time in the Lake District. The cause of this new rebellion was the attempt by a local gentleman to arrest two men who had been leaders of the rebellion there. The angry people of Cumberland attacked Carlisle but were driven away with considerable ferocity by a force of cavalry.

The King's plan had worked – he now had an excuse to move against the rebels, withdraw the promises made by Norfolk and begin the punishment of the ringleaders. The Duke was ordered:

> *to cause such dreadful execution to be done upon a good number of the inhabitants of every town, village and hamlet ... as well by the hanging of them up on trees as by the quartering of them and the setting of their heads and quarters in every town great and small ... as they may be a fearful spectacle to all others hereafter that would practise any like matter.*

> State papers

The Earl of Derby was ordered to Sawley Abbey, where:

> *you shall then, without further delay, cause the said abbot and certain of the chief monks to be hanged upon long pieces of timber out of the steeple, and the rest to be put to execution in such sundry places as you shall think meet for the example of others.*

> State papers

Henry named other monasteries for especially harsh punishment:

> *all these troubles have ensued by the traitorous conspiracies of the monks and canons of those parts.*

> State papers

In total about 200 executions took place, far less than Henry wanted, but, as Norfolk said:

> *the like number hath not been heard to put to execution at any one time.*

> State papers

The most public executions were kept for the two great leaders of the rising, Robert Aske and Lord Darcy. Darcy was arrested on 7 April 1537. To the very end he swore that he was loyal to the King, and he blamed Cromwell for all that had happened:

> *Cromwell, it is thou that art the very original and chief cause of all this rebellion and mischief, and dost daily work to bring us to our end and strike off our heads; and I trust that, though thou wouldst procure all the noblemen's heads within the realm to be struck off, yet shall there one head remain that shall strike off thy head.*

> State papers

*Fountains Abbey,
Yorkshire, at night*

Darcy was beheaded in London, and his head was set upon a spike on London Bridge. Robert Aske was taken to York, where he confessed his sins but would not take back his opinions:

> *He was then laid upon a hurdle and drawn through the main streets of York, desiring the people ever, as he passed by, to pray for him. He was taken to Cliffords Tower and was brought out upon the scaffold on top of the tower, and there he repeated his confession, asking divers times the King's Highness' forgiveness.*

State papers

According to one contemporary source, Aske had especially asked not to be disembowelled while still alive. The King had agreed, but in doing so he commanded that Aske be hanged in chains, a death sentence which would kill him slowly over several days.

The King had shown his power. Aske and his Pilgrimage of Grace were dead.

Using the evidence
As a class exercise discuss why the Pilgrimage of Grace failed. Write up a report in answer to the question.

41

5 THE FALL OF THE GREATER MONASTERIES

One of the aims of the Pilgrimage of Grace had been to save the monasteries. In fact it had served to speed up their final destruction.

We have seen that Henry put the blame for the rebellion on to the monks. Any monk who could be found guilty of treason since the pardon was immediately executed. Most of these came from the smaller monasteries. At Cartmel Priory, which had been restored during the rebellion, 13 monks were sentenced to death. However, there were also larger houses, not yet threatened with closure, which had supported the rebels. One such was Whalley in Lancashire, where the abbot was hanged and his monastery confiscated. Soon after the execution the Abbot of Furness, Abbot Pyle, was summoned to Whalley. He must have been a frightened man, knowing what an important part had been played by his abbey during the rising. He hoped that nothing could be found against him since the pardon, but before leaving for Whalley he called his monks together. He warned them that if the King's officers came:

> they should not meddle with them nor show anything at all to them, or else by Him that made him he should go to prison and never come out.
>
> State papers

But, he was aware that some of his monks could not be trusted, and he arrived at Whalley in fear for his life. There, a discussion with the Earl of Sussex led to an idea which Abbot Pyle snatched at to prove his loyalty to the King. The suggestion was that he should voluntarily surrender Furness Abbey. He signed a document which admitted:

> Knowing the miserable and evil life both unto God and our Prince of the brethren of the said monastery, I do freely and wholly surrender give and grant unto the King's highness the monastery of Furness.
>
> State papers

So it was that the first of the greater monasteries was closed. No Act had been passed. No force was involved. The abbey simply gave itself up. Soon afterwards the abbey at Lewes in Sussex followed suit, and one by one the other great houses surrendered, as well as the smaller monasteries which had survived the 1536 Act.

Rumours that the monasteries were doomed quickly spread. Part of a letter to Lord Lisle from his steward illustrates this point:

> It is thought that most abbeys will go down by consent of their abbots and priors so I trust something will fall to your lordship.
>
> State papers

Some abbots anticipated closure by giving away lands and goods to their friends and patrons. Cromwell quickly wrote to reassure them that there was no plan to close them all:

> *there are malicious and cankered hearts who would persuade and blow abroad a general and violent suppression.*
> *... unless overtures had been made by the houses that have resigned he [the King] would never have received them. He does not intend the suppression of any religious house that standeth, unless they shall desire it themselves, or else misuse themselves contrary to their allegiance.*
>
> State papers

This last sentence gives a clue to the ways in which the government gained surrenders, and can be supported from other sources.

The Abbot of Combermere wrote that he:

> *had his office and the house by the King's Grace and Cromwell's and is ready when it shall please them to take it again.*

The Abbot of St Andrew's, Northamptonshire, wrote:

> *considering their inability to live as they ought, they beg the King to accept the free gift of their house and lands, and to extend his charity to them for livings.*

The Abbot of Pershore, Worcestershire, wrote to Cromwell:

> *I would resign my monastery to the King's Grace and you if it be your pleasure I shall do ... and then give me leave to intreat of my pension, and you to determine it at your pleasure.*
>
> State papers

Question

Is there any explanation in these documents to show why the abbots were willing to surrender their houses?

The last of the greater monasteries

Some abbots were less willing to co-operate. At Montacute, Somerset, the commissioners reported that they:

> *found the Prior in like obstinacy as we had before found the abbot of Bruton, and by so much as by his answer we might suppose that there had been some privy conference between them.*
>
> State papers

The Abbot of St Albans was extremely 'obstinate' saying that he:

would rather choose to beg his bread all the days of his life than consent to surrender.

State papers

However, in all cases the abbots finally gave way. You may have noticed that those who surrendered without any resistance, such as the Abbot of Pershore, were very concerned about pensions. Many abbots, when faced with the promise of a large pension, were persuaded to give way. This also included the Abbots of Montacute, Bruton and St Albans. There remained very few who would not give way. Some, such as the Prioress of Amesbury, resigned their office rather than surrender. Her replacement was to surrender the priory a short time afterwards. Others, in particular the Abbots of Colchester, Reading and Glastonbury, would neither resign nor surrender. Their attitude as expressed by the Abbot of Colchester was that:

the King shall never have my house but against my will and against my heart, for I know by my learning that he cannot take it by right and law.

State papers

The Abbot of Colchester is executed, and the judge moves on

The commissioners also found resistance when they arrived at Glastonbury; they discovered that the abbot would not surrender the abbey, and that he had always stood against the changes made by

Henry VIII until they became law. They returned to examine him again, and as their report shows, to bring greater pressure to bear:

As his answer was not then to our purpose we advised him to call to his remembrance that which he had forgotten and so tell the truth. We visited the abbey and there of new proceeded to search his study for letters and books of arguments against the King's divorce ... and copies of bulls [orders from the Pope]. We examined him again. His answers which we send will show his cankered and traitorous heart.

State papers

Unfortunately the abbot's answers have never been found. However, Cromwell's tactics are easy to see. He had failed to get the surrender so he brought charges against the individual abbots. In the case of the Abbot of Glastonbury the charge was stealing from the abbey. Layton had provided the evidence for this when he reported that they:

*have found money and plate hid in walls, vaults and other secret places, and some conveyed to divers places in the country.
The abbot and monks have embezzled and stolen as much plate and ornaments as would have sufficed for a new abbey.*

State papers

Like the Abbots of Colchester and Reading, the Abbot of Glastonbury suffered a terrible death. He was:

put to execution with two other of his monks for the robbing of Glastonbury church. The said abbot's body being divided into four parts and his head stricken off, whereof one quarter stands at Wells, another at Bath, and at Ilchester and Bridgewater the rest. And the head on the abbey gate at Glastonbury.

State papers

As the abbots had been condemned, their houses fell too. By 1540 the dissolution was complete. To make it all perfectly legal, an act was passed:

Where divers and sundry abbots of their own free and voluntary minds, goodwills and assents, without constraint or compulsion have given, granted and severally confirmed all their said monasteries to our sovereign lord the King and successors for ever.

State papers

Using the evidence
Write a letter from Thomas Cromwell to his commissioners instructing them on how they will proceed with the larger houses: what tactics they should use, and how careful they should be to avoid bad publicity.

The fate of the monks

And in the year of our Lord 1540, the monastery of Evesham was suppressed by King Henry the VIII. The 30th day of January at evensong time, the convent being in the choir at this verse: 'Deposuit Potentes' and the commissioners would not suffer them to make an end.

J. Youings: *The Dissolution of the Monasteries*, 1971

Sir John Uvedale's steward had been there for a week already, making sure that the nuns of Marrick priory carried away nothing but was their own, and having the best of the silver and gold ornaments of the church packed up in canvas, and then in barrels ready to be sent to the King.
It was at about 10 o'clock in the morning that Sir John and his servants came into Swaledale and through the meadows towards Marrick stepping stones. The priory stood opposite them across the river.

An artist's impression of the eviction of nuns

They crossed the stream. Sir John's steward stood in the sunshine; he swung a big key from his finger, the key of the priory gate which the Prioress herself had a moment ago put in his hand.
And now he watched the prioress and the last of her ladies who went with her, and a couple of servants, as they rode into the world.
The steward stood where he was until the ladies were out of sight. Now for the first time for close on four hundred years, there were no nuns at Marrick.

H.F.M. Prescott: Man on a Donkey, 1959

The first extract is a true account of the end of a monastery and the second extract is from a modern novel. It is not hard to imagine the events at Evesham and at Marrick being repeated up and down the country. In the past it had often been believed that the evicted monks and nuns were unable to fend for themselves and that they swelled the already large bands of vagrants. As one historian has pointed out this was especially true of the nuns:

one would not expect a group of women, few of them young, to be anxious to break up their whole way of life and go forth into the unknown.

D. Knowles: The Religious Orders in England, vol. III, 1959

Consider the following evidence concerning the fate of the monks and the nuns.

Eustace Chapuys, the Spanish ambassador, wrote:

It is a lamentable thing to see a legion of monks and nuns who have been chased from their monasteries wandering hither and thither seeking means to live . . . and several honest friends told me there were over 20 000 who knew not how to live.

Spanish papers

The old hermit talks to the young prince about his father, Henry VIII:

Dost know it was he that turned us out into the world houseless and homeless . . . he wrought us evil, he destroyed us and is gone down into the eternal fires.
The King dissolved my religious house, and I poor obscure unfriended monk, was cast homeless upon the world.

Mark Twain: The Prince and the Pauper, 1882

Turned out of their houses, the monks and nuns, especially those to whom no pensions were assigned, must have endured great suffering and undergone many privations in their efforts to gain a livelihood.

Francis Gasquet: Henry VIII and the English Monasteries, 1888

At Dunstable, out of twelve canons, ten can be identified as holding church offices in 1556; at Winchcombe thirteen out of sixteen, at

Hailes sixteen out of twenty, and at St. Augustines Bristol seven out of ten can be found in lucrative employment of one kind or another within a decade or so of the suppression . . . .

The average annual pension for the houses of men was £5. 10s. 0d. In Lincolnshire out of sixty two religious men noted in a county report of 1554, thirty-five had pensions between £5 and £6. 13s. 4d . . . . For women the average was £3 . . . . The pensions were paid with fair regularity by successive governments.

Dom David Knowles: *The Religious Orders in England*, 1959

Using the evidence

1 From these documents, what conclusions can be drawn about the fate of the monks and the nuns? Consider the following points before answering.

   a) Are they all in agreement?

   b) Consider the reliability of each in turn.

      i) Is Chapuys likely to be a reliable witness?

      ii) Of what value is the evidence of the hermit in *The Prince and the Pauper*?

      iii) Gasquet and Knowles are both secondary sources. Is there any reason to believe that one is more reliable than the other?

2 Now write a summary in answer to the question – were monks and nuns able to find a living in the outside world?

Monk Burton Priory

The fate of the monasteries

monasteries of England: on page 26 there is a map of monasteries mentioned in this book. Some have now vanished.

Once the monks were gone, the government intended to demolish the monasteries. Firstly, however, they stripped the buildings of all valuables. Anything saleable was taken out and put up for auction, or if it was very valuable, sent to London for the King's pleasure.

Using the evidence
Items disposed of included:

plate and jewels	pottery and glass
bells	books
lead	livestock
grates, locks etc.	tools
carved woodwork	pans
furniture	vestments
land	stone

Which of these would you have:
a) sent up to London
b) sold at auction
c) melted down and sent to London
d) rented out
e) destroyed as useless

There must have been some amazing bargains at these auctions. At Stafford, a lady bought a table from the brewhouse for 2d., and items for household use must have been almost given away.

The fate of the buildings varied greatly. Here are some examples of what became of the monasteries.

Lewes, Sussex
After the closure of the abbey at Lewes the land was given to Thomas Cromwell's son. Cromwell wanted the buildings to be completely demolished before his son took over there. He hired an Italian expert and 25 men to do the job. They removed stones from the base of the walls, replacing them with timber. Then they set the wood alight, hoping that it would burn away and bring the walls down. Some of the heaviest buttresses stubbornly refused to fall, and the Italian was forced to use explosives. Finally the abbey was flattened, and today nothing is left to remind us of it. A school and a railway line cover the site. Cromwell intended that this should happen to all the abbey buildings, but the cost of demolition was too great, and most buildings were allowed to stand at least for a few more years.

Above: *A carved hand holding a cross, found in a wall at Yarmouth Castle, Isle of Wight*
Right: *St Mawes, Cornwall. The Tudor badge can still be seen*

Abbeys of the south coast

In the early chapters of this book we saw that one very important reason for the closure of the monasteries was to pay for Henry's personal extravagance, including his wars. Ironically, some of the abbey buildings were also used for war.

Henry built a series of massive coastal forts. These castles, such as Deal, Sandgate and St Mawes, each cost about £27 000 to build. The stone, however, came cheap. In the walls of Yarmouth Castle, Isle of Wight, a sculpted hand can be seen holding a cross. This reminds us that the castle walls were built of stone from nearby abbeys.

Merton Abbey

A document still exists today which shows what happened to the buildings of Merton Abbey:

Paid to John Whytaker for uncovering the body of the church at Merton Abbey.

Carriage of Stone from Merton Abbey, 4 miles at 2d. the mile, 8d. per load of 20 cwt.

> *April – May – 350 loads*
> *May – June – 500 loads*
> *June – July – 1300 loads*
> *July – August – 500 loads*
> *August – September – 400 loads*

State papers

It sounds as if every stone of Merton Abbey was being transported to the new site. But for what purpose? To find the answer we need look no further than the King. Henry had come to the moment of his greatest personal extravagance. Merton Abbey was being carried away, stone by stone, to a park in Cheam, Surrey, where Henry planned to build as never before:

> *Only a King could have commandeered the site, found the money, and enrolled such diverse teams of artists and craftsmen.*
>
> J. Gloag: *The English Tradition in Architecture*, 1963

An historian of architecture wrote of his plans:

> *Not only his contemporaries, but also posterity should be witness to his magnificence. Some two thousand acres of prime estate were swept clean to make way for the greatest palace in England, a monument that would stand comparison with the finest in Europe – in the world for that matter – and which would bear a name to match – Nonsuch.*
>
> Lacey Baldwin Smith: *Henry VIII*, 1971

> *[Nonsuch Palace,] a building flanked by tall octagonal towers which splayed outward as they rose above the roof line of the main structure. Nonsuch, with its lofty angle towers and pinnacles and cupolas was an architectural freak ... it was like a King's palace in a pantomime.*
>
> J. Gloag: *The English Tradition in Architecture*, 1963

Nonsuch Palace

There has never been anything else quite like it. Sadly, it was destroyed in 1682, and although archaeologists have uncovered the foundations, there is nothing left above ground level.

Fountains Abbey

Lewes and Merton have gone. Fountains, like many other abbeys in lonely parts of the country, is still with us. The roof has gone and some parts of the abbey have weathered and collapsed. Some of the stone, from the dormitory, was removed to build nearby Fountains Hall. As for the rest, it was sturdily built with thick walls and great buttresses. For centuries the walls stood proudly but uncared for, until in modern times their value was realised and they were properly treated. You can visit Fountains Abbey today – or Furness, Tintern, Sweetheart and others – and marvel at the way they have survived the test of time. With a little imagination we can look at these ruins and reconstruct the life of the monks who lived there over 500 years ago.

Buckland Abbey. Sir Francis Drake's home, but unmistakeably once a monastery. How can you tell that it has been both house and church?

Buckland Abbey

Many abbeys were neither pulled down nor allowed to collapse, but were converted into homes which have survived to this day. When Buckland Abbey was closed the property was bought by Sir Richard

Grenville. The buildings were undisturbed for 30 years, until Sir Richard's grandson decided to convert the house. By removing one wall and building on a kitchen, and by constructing two floors and dividing them into rooms, he made himself a unique home. The house is more famous today because its next owner was Sir Francis Drake, and it is now a museum of Drake's life. However, there are constant reminders that it was once a monastery: the outside walls; the chapel, once the site of the high altar; the beautiful sculpted archways, once abbey windows but now strange room dividers; and the great tithe barn, where once the abbey grain was stored.

Chester Cathedral

Abbeys such as Buckland are still used, but not for the purpose that was intended, namely, the worship of God. However, a small number of monastery buildings are still in use today as places of worship. These were the abbeys which became either churches, or cathedrals as was the case at Westminster, Gloucester and Chester. The abbey at Chester was made into a cathedral in 1540. A bishop was appointed to serve there, and to run the newly created diocese. Over the years some changes have been made to the abbey buildings, but there is no better place to see what a monastery was like. Beautiful stonework and

Chester Cathedral

sculpture and elaborate wooden carvings decorate the cathedral and the other monastery buildings. Looking at the beauty of Chester Cathedral it is possible to recognise the enormity of England's architectural loss brought about by the destruction of the monasteries.

Using the evidence

Earlier in this book you have completed flow diagrams. Now construct a flow diagram of your own to show the fate of the monastery buildings. Try to add what happened to any monasteries near to where you live. Either add them to the categories already described or, if they had a different fate, create a new category.

EPILOGUE

By January 1547, it was evident that Henry VIII was dying. His anger still created terror, so his doctors were too scared to tell him. Finally, a gentleman of the court 'told him what case he was in, and exhorted him to prepare himself to death'. The King called for Thomas Cranmer, Archbishop of Canterbury, his oldest and most respected servant. Unable to speak, Henry wrung Cranmer's hand and then died, sure to the end of God's mercy.

The Chancellor waited two days before announcing the King's death, and even then could hardly hold back his tears. The whole country went into mourning, and the funeral procession to Windsor stretched for miles. The mourners could look back on a magnificent reign — one of splendour and glory. Truly this had been a remarkable king, one for history to remember.

However, there were some who did not mourn him. One of these was the man who, nearly 40 years before, had been a young monk at Cartmel Priory. To think that he had prayed for the new king on the day of his coronation! Now he cursed the soul of this king who had destroyed Cartmel and many other abbeys and their treasures. He was glad that Henry VIII was dead!

A propaganda picture in Henry's old age. Note Henry's youthful face, men destroying Catholic images and the Pope being destroyed by the true word of God

Using the evidence

What do you think of King Henry VIII? Make out an argument for or against him, supported by reasons and examples drawn from his reign.

INDEX

Numbers in **bold** denote illustrations